Richard Armour's Punctured Poems

Famous First and Infamous Second Lines

By
Richard Armour

Illustrated by
Eric Gurney

Woodbridge Press / *Santa Barbara, California*

Published and distributed by

Woodbridge Press Publishing Company
Post Office Box 6189
Santa Barbara, California 93111

Published simultaneously in the United States and Canada.

Library of Congress Cataloging in Publication Data

Armour, Richard Willard, 1906-
Richard Armour's Punctured Poems.

1. Parodies. I. Gurney, Eric. II. Title.
III. Title: Punctured poems.
PS3501.R55P8 1982 811'.52 82-10989
ISBN 0-912800-55-0 (Formerly 07-002293-3, McGraw-Hill)

ACKNOWLEDGMENTS

I am indebted to the many great writers without whose famous first lines this book would have been only half as long. My thanks also go to Martin Levin, who originally published a few of these first-and-second lines in "The Phoenix Nest" of the *Saturday Review*, and to Francis Coughlin, who thought up several truly infamous lines, one of which appears on the cover.

FOREWORD

Most of these famous first lines are the first lines of famous poems. The reason the first line is usually more famous than the rest of the poem is that most people do not read any farther. Besides, by quoting the first line and saying "and so forth" they get credit for having read and remembered the whole poem, thus accomplishing their objective.

However, some of these famous first lines are not the first lines of poems. They are somewhere in the middle or near the end. How such lines became famous is a mystery. One theory is that poets originally wrote them as the first line and then moved them down to another place so that teachers could find out whether students had read that far.

Even when the famous first lines are not the first lines of famous poems, they are famous first lines. That is, they are the first of two lines, and they are more famous than the second lines, or at least they have been up to now. In time, the second lines may become more famous than the first, which will make possible the publication of another book, subtitled *Famous Second and Infamous First Lines*. It will be identical with the present volume, and the reader who does not wish to buy both books may simply buy the two titles, which may be used interchangeably. Offhand, it is hard to think of anything comparable in the literary world.

Occasionally a famous first line will not strike the reader as famous. The reader may insist he has never heard of it, and he may be right. But this is not the fault of the poet who wrote the line or the compiler who included it in this book. It is the fault of the reader, who skipped some of the assignments in English 56a,b, Great English and American Poets, knowing there wouldn't be a question on *everything.*

No apologies are made for the infamous second lines. Some of them will seem better when read over and over. At least they will approximately offset the number of lines which seem worse. If the reader is still unhappy, he can cross out the offending line and write something of his own—if it is not a borrowed copy.

It is a good idea to read only a few of these lines at one sitting. From time to time the reader should stand up and walk around. If he walks very far, he may not come back. That is a gamble the author has to take.

R.A.

Leigh Hunt, "Rondeau"

Jenny kissed me when we met.
Not oft such quick results I get.[1]

[1] According to one theory, kissing goes back to the craving of prehistoric man for salt. After trying various places, he found the heaviest deposits on women's lips. In the early days, a woman who had been kissed was said to have lost her salinity. But she gradually got it back.

William Blake, "The Tiger"

Tiger! Tiger! burning bright,
What has caused you to ignite?

GIN
Schwepp
E Gurney

Anonymous, "Cuckoo Song"

Sumer is icumen in;
Mix the tonic and the gin.[1]

[1] After a few drinks, it becomes easier to sing "Cuccu! cuccu! cuccu!" In this connection, see Wordsworth's

O Cuckoo! shall I call thee bird?
I can't think of a better word.

John Greenleaf Whittier, "Barbara Frietchie"

"Shoot, if you must, this old gray head.
I've had it long enough," she said.[1]

[1] Whittier himself would have had trouble holding a gun without his hand shaking. He was a Quaker. It was Whittier, in a gentler mood, who wrote:

> Maud Muller on a summer's day
> Raked. She should of left it lay.

Felicia Hemans, "Casabianca"

The boy stood on the burning deck.
He'd sat, but got up quick, by heck.

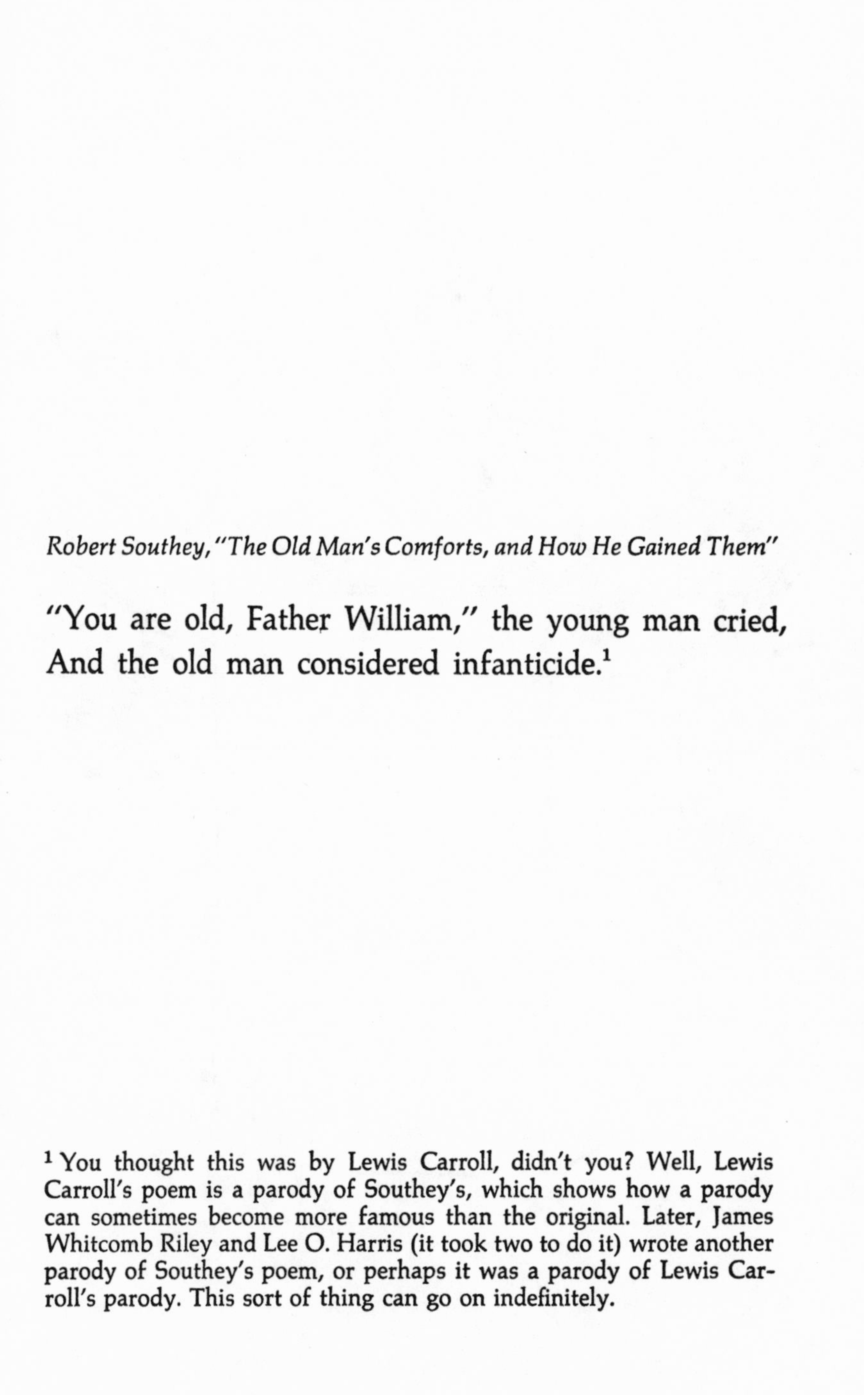

Robert Southey, "The Old Man's Comforts, and How He Gained Them"

"You are old, Father William," the young man cried,
And the old man considered infanticide.[1]

[1] You thought this was by Lewis Carroll, didn't you? Well, Lewis Carroll's poem is a parody of Southey's, which shows how a parody can sometimes become more famous than the original. Later, James Whitcomb Riley and Lee O. Harris (it took two to do it) wrote another parody of Southey's poem, or perhaps it was a parody of Lewis Carroll's parody. This sort of thing can go on indefinitely.

Edmund Waller, "On a Girdle"

That which her slender waist confined
Now, though she tugs, won't meet behind.[1]

[1] Waller, whose dates were 1606-87, envied young men whose dates were 36-23-36.

Elizabeth Akers Allen, "Rock Me to Sleep"

Backward, turn backward, O Time, in your flight,
And it will be yesterday morning tonight.[1]

[1] This will be understood by anyone who understands Daylight Saving Time.

WALT WHITMAN

Walt Whitman, "Song of Myself"

I celebrate myself, and sing myself.
My picture's there, my bust's upon the shelf.[1]

[1] Nor should we forget Whitman's "I Hear America Singing":
I hear America singing, the varied carols I hear.
The doctor thinks maybe something is loose in my inner ear.

John Donne, "Song"

Go and catch a falling star,
And if you miss the first, that's par.[1]

[1] You, may preferre the originall punctuatione and spellinge:
Goe, and catche a falling starre.

Thomas Moore, "Believe Me, If All Those Endearing Young Charms"

Believe me, if all those endearing young charms
Were removed from your bracelet, I *might* see your
  arms.

John Milton, "On His Blindness"

When I consider how my light is spent,
I'm glad utilities come with the rent.[1]

[1] An even more pathetic poem is Milton's "Lycidas." These lines will show why:

> Yet once more, O ye laurels, and once more,
> Once more, once more (the needle's stuck), once more. . . .

Alexander Pope, "Essay on Man"

Lo, the poor Indian! whose untutor'd mind
Can barely add his oil wells, all combined.[1]

[1] Have you ever heard of an Indian named Lo? More likely he was Chinese, or an Indian of Chinese ancestry whose forebears came over by the Bering Strait. As for the Indian's untutored mind, it was also Pope who, still worried about education, said in his *Essay on Criticism:*

"A little learning is a dangerous thing,"
The dropout muttered, leaving school last spring.

Sir Walter Scott, "Marmion"

Oh, what a tangled web we weave!
The webs to spiders we should leave.[1]

[1] Readers who labor through *Ivanhoe* don't know how lucky they are. Scott might have written it in verse.

W.T.K.
PLUMBER

Samuel Taylor Coleridge, "The Rime of the Ancient Mariner"

Water, water, everywhere;
The plumbing badly needs repair.

Robert Burns, "A Red, Red Rose"

Oh, my love is like a red, red rose,
And her thorns have scratched me on the nose.[1]

[1] In the original it's not "love" but "luve." However, this made little difference to Burns. He might, had he thought of them, have written the lines:

I'd rather far have lived like me
Than won the village spelling bee.

William Congreve, "The Mourning Bride"

Music hath charms to soothe the savage breast;
That's why I keep a flute tucked in my vest.

Rudyard Kipling, "Danny Deever"

They've taken of his buttons off an' cut his stripes
away,
An' if they go on cuttin', he'll be naked as a jay.[1]

[1] Kipling was a manly type, most at home somewhere (somewheres) east of Suez, in a barracks with other he-men. When he chanced to think of women, he was inclined to make invidious comparisons, as in "The Betrothed":

> A woman is only a woman, but a good cigar is a smoke.
> Though a woman's not made of tobacco, she's often
> the butt of the joke.

Alfred Noyes, "The Highwayman"

The moon was a ghostly galleon tossed upon cloudy
seas,
And I cried, looking up, "While you're tossing,
don't toss out your anchor, please!"[1]

[1] Emily Dickinson also had rather far-out ideas about sailing vessels. "There is no frigate like a book," she writes, and one wonders whether it ever occurred to her how soggy the pages would get.

Alexander Pope, "Moral Essays"

Who shall decide when doctors disagree?
The undertaker, very probably.[1]

[1] One of the most famous doctors in literature is Doctor Fell, described by Thomas Brown in his "Written While a Student at Christ Church, Oxford." Tom should have been studying instead of writing things like this:

I do not love thee, Doctor Fell.
The reason is, you charge like hell.

To be honest about it, Doctor Fell was not an M.D. but a D.D., and Dean of Christ Church, Oxford. However, he liked to be called Doctor, like Doctor Samuel Johnson, as long as no one got him up at 3:00 A.M. to set a broken leg.

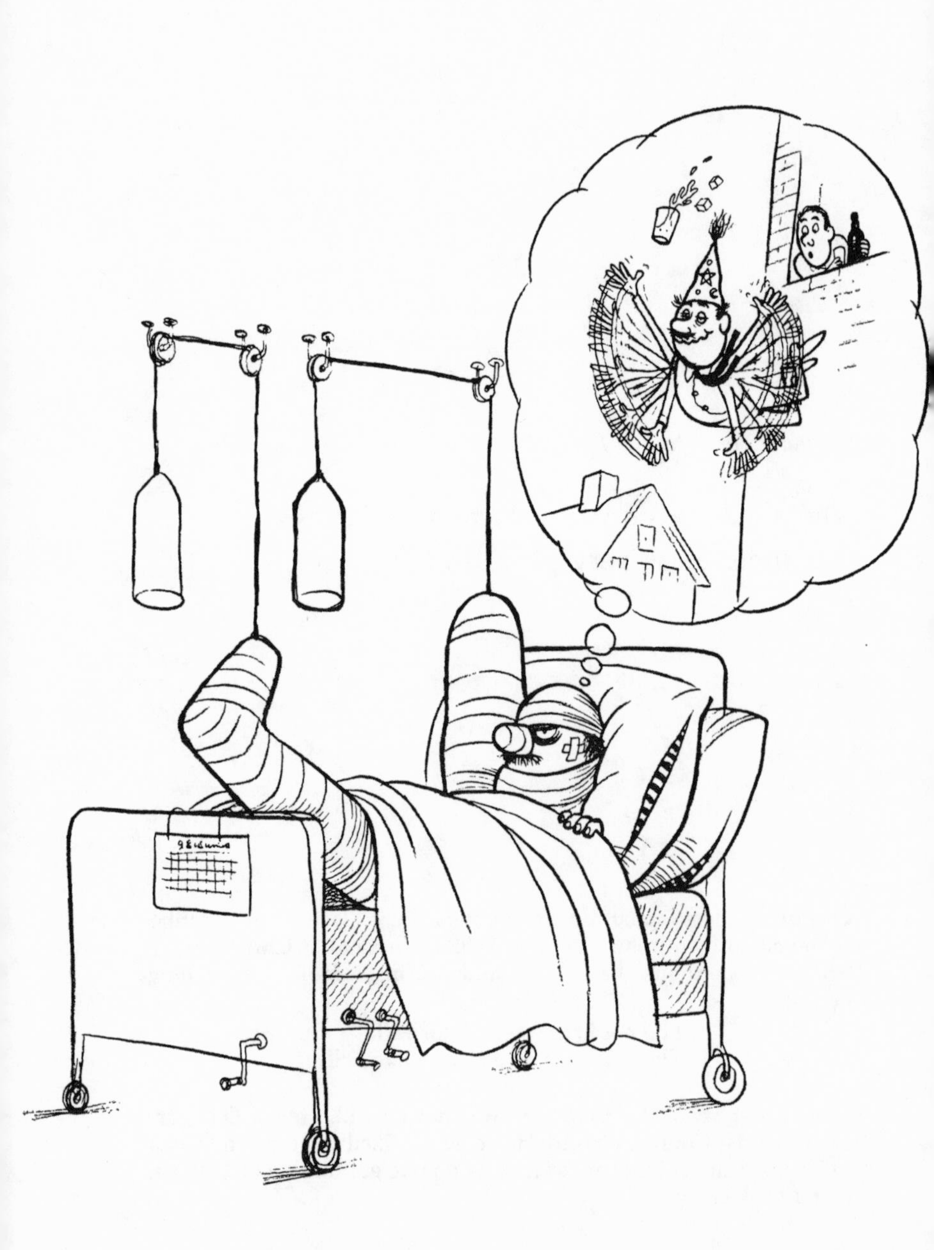

Edgar A. Guest, "It Couldn't Be Done"

Somebody said that it couldn't be done,
And the fellow was right, the son of a gun.[1]

[1] Guest also wrote those lines which have inspired many a sufferer from anemia: "It takes a heap o' liver. . . ."

Henry Wadsworth Longfellow, "Paul Revere's Ride"

One if by land, and two if by sea....
Now what do I do? He signals three![1]

[1] As Longfellow says in his poem, written in 1863, "Hardly a man is now alive" to remember this perplexing incident. After all, it occurred on April 18, 1775. Even fewer are alive today to recall it. It was not Longfellow but Irene Warsaw, in a poem in her book, *A Word in Edgewise* (The Golden Quill Press), who wrote the touching line: "I shot an error into the air."

Percy Bysshe Shelley, "The Cloud"

I bring fresh showers for the thirsting flowers.
I've stood in the sun, with a hose, for hours.[1]

[1] See also Thomas Edward Brown's

> A garden is a lovesome thing, God wot,
> But only if God wotters it a lot.

This somehow calls to mind Thomas Campion's

> There is a garden in her face;
> She uses every inch of space.

William Wordsworth, "Character of the Happy Warrior"

Who is the happy Warrior? Who is he
But one sent home, a scratch upon his knee.[1]

[1] More characteristic of Wordsworth, a nature lover, is his

One impulse from a vernal wood
Is not enough to do much good.

Some critics think these apparently simple lines are fraught with hidden meaning, and the poet is referring to a friend named A. Vernal Wood.

Sir John Suckling, "Why So Pale and Wan?"

Why so pale and wan, fond lover?
She cannot cook, you now discover?

Robert Browning, "My Last Duchess"

That's my last Duchess painted on the wall.
I've scraped, but cannot get her off at all.[1]

[1] "My Last Duchess" is a dramatic monologue, and therefore should be read dramatically in a monotonous monotone. It was Browning, no ornithologist, who wrote "The lark's on the wing," when it obviously should have been "The wing's on the lark." As for "The snail's on the thorn," it could be either way.

HERS
HIS

Ernest Dowson, "A Valediction"

If we must part, then let it be like this:
You keep the stuff marked HERS, I'll take the HIS.

Isaac Watts, "Divine Songs"

How doth the little busy bee
Improve? By practicing on me.[1]

[1] Of the many parodies of "How doth the little busy bee," one I especially like (because I wrote it) is "Bee Lines," based on a news item to the effect that "Russian experts claim to have trained bees to seek nectar and pollen from specific plants and to ignore others." It opens:

How doth the regimented bee
  Improve each shining hour?
He flies to each selected tree
  And designated flower.

And it closes:

No longer flying fancy-free,
  No longer ranging bold . . .
How doth the regimented bee?
  He doth as he is told.

The whole thing will be found in *Light Armour,* available in your favorite bookstore (and mine).

William Wordsworth, "Lucy Gray"

Oft I had heard of Lucy Gray,
And what I heard I'd best not say.[1]

[1] Perhaps it was something sexy, such as this, which Wordsworth says elsewhere:

> The child is father of the man.
> One wonders how it all began.

PAT. 7325681

Alexander Pope, "Essay on Criticism"

To err is human, to forgive divine.
Some errors I forgive, though, quickly.
. . . Mine.[1]

[1] And then there is Charles Townsend Copeland's "To eat is human; to digest, divine."

Oliver Goldsmith, "The Vicar of Wakefield"

When lovely woman stoops to folly
In low-cut gown, men murmur, "Golly!"[1]

[1] A low-cut gown is, to paraphrase Shakespeare, "the kindest cut of all."

R.I.P.

John Keats, "When I Have Fears"

When I have fears that I may cease to be,
I think: "I'll have a lot of company."[1]

[1] Even more famous, from "Ode on a Grecian Urn," is

Beauty is truth, truth beauty—that is all
Of Keats's poem many can recall.

Keats had a dictionary in which, when he looked up "beauty," it said "See truth," and when he looked up "truth," it said "See beauty." He spent hours going back and forth. No wonder he died young.

OUT WEST

Sir Walter Scott, "Lochinvar"

O, young Lochinvar is come out of the west;
With Greeley's advice he was quite unimpressed.

Omar Khayyám (tr. by Edward FitzGerald), "Rubáiyát"

A jug of wine, a loaf of bread, and thou. . . .
I'm not so very hungry anyhow.[1]

[1] In the same poem we also have:

> The moving finger writes and, having writ,
> Is badly stained with ink, you must admit.

This is one way to save wear and tear on your fountain pen, though it makes a rather broad script.

Robert W. Service, "The Law of the Yukon"

This is the Law of the Yukon, that only the Strong
  shall thrive,
And only the Warmest Blooded are likely to stay
  alive.

Robert Louis Stevenson, "My Shadow"

I have a little shadow that goes in and out with me.
It's only when it's dark that I've the slightest privacy.

LLOYD'S OF LONDON
CEMENT

William Shakespeare, "The Tempest"

Full fathom five thy father lies.
I pushed him. I apologize.[1]

[1] Let us not neglect Shakespeare's sonnets. For instance there is the one called "XXX," which probably had a more meaningful title until Shakespeare crossed it out. This contains the oft-quoted lines:

> When to the sessions of sweet silent thought
> I come—alas, I often think of nought.

Study that first line. Seldom has Shakespeare been so spendthrift of sibilants.

Eugene Field, "Little Boy Blue"

The little toy dog is covered with dust.
As a housekeeper, Mother, I fear you're a bust.[1]

[1] One of Field's poems, about a gingham dog and a calico cat who eat each other up, poses a problem for the S.P.C.A. Then there is his "Wynken, Blynken, and Nod," which those who have read it say is not about a law firm.

Robert Browning, "How They Brought the Good News from Ghent to Aix" [1]

I sprang to the stirrup, and Joris, and he;
I sat upon Joris, the third guy on me.[2]

[1] "Aix" rhymes with "ex," as in the expression "Aix marks the spot."
[2] See the Ritz Brothers in "Three Men on a Horse."

Alfred, Lord Tennyson, "In Memoriam" [1]

'Tis better to have loved and lost
Than married someone and been bossed.[2]

[1] Alfred, who was not only Lord Tennyson but Baron of Aldworth and Farringford, had almost as many titles as his poems.

[2] Tennyson himself was cautious, not marrying until he was forty. There is no evidence that he ever had an illegitimate child, like Wordsworth, or an incestuous relationship, like Byron. But scholars keep looking and hoping.

Christopher Marlowe, "Dr. Faustus"

Was this the face that launch'd a thousand ships?
No wonder there are keel marks on her lips.[1]

[1] Helen of Troy is said to have had a full lower lip. Apparently it was full of bolts and barnacles.

A.A.

Gelett Burgess, "The Purple Cow"

I never saw a Purple Cow
Or pink one, once I took the vow.

Robert Frost, "Mending Wall"

Something there is that doesn't love a wall;
For instance, batted against it oft, a ball.[1]

[1] There is something earthy about Frost's poetry. One of his earthiest is "The Pasture":

> I'm going out to clean the pasture spring;
> The health authorities condemned the thing.

But Frost also has his gay, imaginative side, as in "Birches":

> When I see birches bend to left and right,
> I'm on a bender and am slightly tight.

LUNCHROOM

T. S. Eliot, "The Hollow Men"

We are the hollow men.
It's time to eat again.[1]

[1] Or, in view of the capital in some texts:
We are the Hollow men:
Fred Hollow, Bert Hollow, Ben.

AND A FEW EXTRA

Geoffrey Chaucer, "The Canterbury Tales"
Whan that Aprille with his shoures sote
Hath come, it takes the crease from pants and cote.

Anonymous, "Back and Side Go Bare, Go Bare"
Back and side go bare, go bare;
Wear clothes in front, though, here and there.

Edmund Spenser, "The Faerie Queene"
A Gentle Knight was pricking on the plaine.
The steede he prick'd (with pinne) thought him insane.

Ben Jonson, "To Celia"
Drink to me only with thine eyes.
It's hard to do, I realize.

Edna St. Vincent Millay, "Figs from Thistles"
My candle burns at both ends.
Where can I set it down, my friends?

Dante Gabriel Rossetti, "The Blessed Damozel"
The blessed damozel leaned out.
"She's sick!" I heard a warning shout.

George Gordon, Lord Byron, "The Prisoner of Chillon"
My hair is gray, but not with years;
No, just with dissipation, dears.

Robert Burns, "My Heart's in the Highlands"
My heart's in the highlands, my heart is not here;
All the doctors are puzzled, they think it is queer.

John Keats, "On the Grasshopper and Cricket"
Pillow'd upon my fair love's ripening breast,
When she exhaled, I was a bit depressed.

James Whitcomb Riley, "Little Orphant Annie"
Little Orphant Annie's come to our house to stay,
An' soon she'll be a-learnin', too, to speak this silly way.

Alfred, Lord Tennyson, "Sir Galahad"
My strength is as the strength of ten.
Just watch me crush my fountain pen.

Sara Teasdale, "The Look"
Strephon kissed me in the spring.
It squeaked. I'll have to oil the thing.

Edwin Markham, "The Man with the Hoe"
Bowed by the weight of centuries he leans.
Some day his hoe will break to smithereens.

Thomas Dunn English, "Ben Bolt"
Don't you remember sweet Alice, Ben Bolt?
If you saw her today, Ben, she'd give you a jolt.

James Russell Lowell, "The Present Crisis"
Once to every man and nation comes the moment to decide.
Came the moment. He was braced for it. "Well, yes and no," he cried.